Original title:
Lost in the Fire

Copyright © 2024 Book Fairy Publishing
All rights reserved.

Editor: Theodor Taimla
Author: Meelis Maurus
ISBN HARDBACK: 978-9916-756-42-3
ISBN PAPERBACK: 978-9916-756-43-0

Glow of Yesterday

In twilight's hush, the memories rise,
Faded echoes from the sky.
Golden hues of days long passed,
In our hearts, forever cast.

Silent whispers in the breeze,
Tales of joy among the trees.
Laughter light and shadows play,
In the glow of yesterday.

Fields of dreams where we would roam,
Every step a journey home.
Moments stitched in time's grand loom,
Petals bright in endless bloom.

Evening stars now softly gleam,
Guardians of each tender dream.
Though the past may drift away,
In our souls, the light will stay.

Pyro's Path

Through embers' gleam, the way is paved,
A trail of fire, relentless, brave.
Flames dance along the crimson path,
In twilight's gaze, where shadows bathe.

Scorched earth beneath the wanderer's feet,
A journey wrought in searing heat.
The whisper of the burning night,
Guides the soul to dawn's first light.

Where cinders wane and ashes fall,
A tale unfolds in fire's thrall.
Step fast through forge, no hint of wrath,
For truth lies in the Pyro's Path.

Shimmering Void

In the expanse of midnight's flare,
Stars form whispers in the air.
A boundless sea of endless night,
Where dreams take wing in void's soft light.

Nebulae, in hues untamed,
Conceal the secrets stars have claimed.
Through cosmic drift, where silence reigns,
Echoes of the ancient chains.

Glimmering waves of starlit tide,
Reveal the tales the void can't hide.
Beauty in the endless ploy,
Behold, the Shimmering Void.

Combustive Emotions

Passions spark in fervent blaze,
Hearts ignite in mystic craze.
From depths of soul, desires spring,
Combustive fuel, their song to sing.

Eyes like flames in darkened night,
Heat exchanged, a rare delight.
Unseen yet felt, the burning ties,
Beneath the sky where love complies.

Eruptions in the silent space,
Feelings dart, they weave, they race.
Binding two through passion's motions,
Lost within combustive emotions.

Fuel of Forgotten

In shadows cast by time's own hand,
Lie whispers of a distant land.
The echoes of long-silent dreams,
Fuel of forgotten, ever gleams.

Memories buried deep in ash,
Fragments in a fleeting flash.
From embered past, a spark is caught,
Reviving what the years forgot.

Through smoky veils, the old light shines,
Stirring souls with ancient lines.
From history's grain, a story gotten,
Rekindled by the fuel of forgotten.

Resonance of the Flame

Flickering light in twilight's breath,
Whispering secrets of birth and death.
Shadows dance with a fervent plea,
In fire's embrace, the soul runs free.

Ancient echoes, the embers hold,
Stories of passion, fierce and bold.
Heat sings softly a timeless song,
Binding hearts where they belong.

From sparks of life to ashes grey,
Flame's sweet agony leads the way.
Memories burn bright, then wane,
In resonance, we feel the flame.

Conflagrant Echo

Blaze within a quiet night,
Setting stars with a muted light.
Echoes of fire in silence break,
A symphony no heart can fake.

Inferno whispers through the air,
A call to dreamers everywhere.
Timeless dance on a charred stage,
Resonates beyond age.

Flames in echoes, words unwritten,
In this hush, the sparks get smitten.
Silent yet loud, the conflagrant call,
Binds us, frees us, consumes us all.

Evanescent Heat

Fleeting warmth in cold night's shroud,
Passion whispers, never loud.
A touch of fire, so brief, so sweet,
Dissolving in the silence, evanescent heat.

Moments blaze then gently fade,
In glowing embers, dreams are laid.
Heat's tender touch, so quick to flee,
Leaves behind a longing plea.

In shadows deep, where fires recede,
Love's own hunger finds its need.
A transient kiss, a soft retreat,
The essence of the evanescent heat.

Desolation's Glow

In barren lands where silence reigns,
A single flame, the night sustains.
Lonely ember, glowing fierce,
Through desolation, it pierces.

Ghostly whispers through the ash,
Memories of a fiery crash.
Still, the glow remains to show,
Through demise, a burning woe.

Bare and empty, yet it shines,
In desolation, hope aligns.
From the darkness, light does grow,
The bittersweet of desolation's glow.

Remains of Passion

In shadows long, where whispers play,
Two hearts once danced, now led astray.
A lingering scent, a fading dream,
Of love once bright, now just a gleam.

The fire's warmth that once was shared,
Leaves traces faint but still declared.
Memories etched in twilight's hues,
A silent song of love we lose.

Through moonlit nights, the embers glow,
Of fleeting love, time will not slow.
Yet in the dawn, the truth remains,
Passion's echoes in our veins.

Ignited Void

In the void where stars once gleamed,
A spark ignites what once was dreamed.
A blazing path through empty night,
Guided by an unseen light.

Through silent space, the fire roars,
Breaking past the cosmic doors.
A universe of dark concessions,
Illuminated by obsessions.

Beyond the reach of mortal sight,
A dance of flame against the night.
The void now whispers, fiercely bright,
Consumed by passion, burning tight.

Flame-kissed Regrets

In the stillness of the night,
A candle burns with gentle light.
Each flicker tells a tale of yore,
Of love pursued and hearts once sore.

The warmth once held in tender glance,
Now scorched by fate's unyielding dance.
Regrets lay bare in ember's glow,
Of paths we took, we'll never know.

Upon the hearth where memories sit,
A silent film, regrets emit.
Yet through the ash of yesterday,
Hope flickers, finding its way.

Sultry Echoes

In the heat of summer's breath,
Where days stretch long, defying death.
A whisper soft, a sultry plea,
Carries echoes through the tree.

Beneath the sun's relentless fire,
Desires burn, tempers inspire.
Sweat and sighs, a fervent trance,
Nature's call to love's advance.

As the dusk begins to fall,
Shadows lengthen, whispers call.
Sultry echoes, passion's song,
Through the night, it lingers on.

Scorched Reflections

In the mirror, flames do dance,
Casting shadows, a somber trance;
Eyes that once knew gentle light,
Now gleam with embers through the night.

Silent whispers, cracks and pops,
Memories burn in endless loops;
Each flicker past, a tale entombs,
Of tender hearts, consumed in gloom.

Ashes fall like snowflakes gray,
Marking paths where love once lay;
Scorched reflections, truths untold,
In fiery depths, secrets unfold.

The Blaze Within

Heartbeats forge a fierce embrace,
Fueling dreams in scorching pace;
Blaze within, a soul ignites,
Banishes the coldest nights.

Passion's fire, rare and pure,
Burns through shadows, tempests cure;
Whispers warmth to silent fears,
Lights the path through darkest years.

Every spark, a guiding star,
Raging wild yet tender scar;
In each ember, tales begin,
Timeless fires lie within.

Hearts Afire

Two hearts meet in searing glance,
In the heat, they start to dance;
Underneath a sky so red,
Love's ignited, passions spread.

Flames twist through each whispered word,
Silent songs of warmth unheard;
Burning bright, their fates align,
In that blaze, their spirits shine.

Kindred souls in fiery clasp,
Strengthen bonds with every gasp;
In this furnace, fears retire,
Warmed eternally, hearts afire.

Hearts Adrift

Two ships sail on waves of flame,
Bound by neither time nor name;
In oceans wide, their paths do swerve,
Fates and fires, intertwined curves.

From the embers, stories soar,
Hearts adrift seek distant shores;
Guided by a burning thread,
Ancient dreams they chase ahead.

In the tempest, love endures,
Blazing trails through endless tours;
Undeterred by rising rift,
In warm currents, hearts adrift.

Eternal Char

In the hearth of yesterday,
Embers warm the cold decay;
Fires once, now whispers far,
Left behind, an eternal char.

Memories in smoke do rise,
Painted in the twilight skies;
Fleeting moments, brief yet bright,
Burnt into the endless night.

Ashes tell of battles won,
Of the setting and the sun;
In the heart where fires scar,
Lingers still, an eternal char.

Inferno Illusions

In dreams of fire, my heart does yearn,
For flames that dance, and embers burn,
In shadows cast by this desire,
My soul's consumed by phantom fire.

The sparks ignite a blazing screen,
Where truth and myth collide, convene,
In this inferno's cruel design,
Reality and dreams entwine.

Within the heat, confusion swells,
A burning maze of molten wells,
I wander lost in scorching blaze,
Ensnared within this fiery haze.

Yet, in the flames I find my way,
Led by the light of breaking day,
Inferno's grip at last released,
From flaming chains, my soul's at peace.

Scorching Reveries

In deserts vast, where sunbeams lie,
My thoughts take flight, beneath the sky,
A mirage forms in heat's embrace,
A reverie in burning space.

The sands of time, they flow and burn,
With every grain, my dreams return,
A blazing path through dunes of gold,
Where stories of the past unfold.

A wistful breeze, both fierce and warm,
Sweeps through my mind, a spectral storm,
In scorching reverie's mystic glow,
I follow where the phantoms go.

The echoes of a heated dream,
Resound within this endless gleam,
With every step, the past ignites,
Till dusk calms down these wayward lights.

Singed Stories

In smoke-strewn skies, where embers drift,
Lie tales of love and hope and rift,
A parchment singed by time's cruel hand,
Each story etched in burning sand.

Beneath the cinders, whispers rise,
Of ancient wounds and silent cries,
A narrative of flame and ash,
Where souls once burned in passion's flash.

Each singed tale a fiery thread,
Connecting hearts both lost and red,
In every spark, a past revives,
Through burning lines, our history thrives.

Though ashes now may cloak the text,
The essence lingers, unperplexed,
These singed stories, forever bright,
Illumine paths in darkest night.

Phoenix of Sorrow

From ashes born, in twilight's grief,
Rises a bird, from burning leaf,
A phoenix forged by sorrow's flame,
To seek anew, and start the same.

Its wings afire with mournful hues,
In every beat, a sadness brews,
A flight of tears through evening's shade,
Where memories, and hopes, cascade.

Yet, through the sorrow, strength is found,
In fiery rebirth, no chains are bound,
This phoenix soars beyond despair,
In every loss, a strength so rare.

For though it rises from lament,
Its heart with future dreams is bent,
The Phoenix of Sorrow spreads its flame,
Reborn through grief, in love's own name.

Flickering Goodbyes

In the quiet dusk, where shadows play,
Memories whisper and gently sway,
Flickers of moments, bright and brief,
Fade to darkness, we find our grief.

Paths once converged, now drift apart,
Echoes of laughter, a tender heart,
Embrace the silence, hold it tight,
Within the night, dreams take flight.

Stars may guide us, through the night,
Casting shadows, soft and slight,
But the dawn brings light anew,
Fading farewells in morning dew.

Embers of Desolation

Burning quietly in the dark,
Silent as the night's stark,
Embers whisper tales of woe,
Forgotten dreams in their glow.

Ashes float on gentle breezes,
Grieving hearts bear silent sieges,
Desolation, cold and wide,
Haunts the embers, where souls hide.

Hope may rise on wings of dawn,
Chasing shadows, sorrow gone,
But in the heart, embers stay,
A silent fire, guiding the way.

Burned Bridges

Over streams where shadows dance,
Bridges burned by fate and chance,
Smoke ascends in spiraled grace,
Echoes lost in time and space.

Once we crossed on paths of gold,
Stories shared, both young and old,
Now those beams lie charred and bare,
Silent witness to the air.

With each step, we move away,
From the ruins of yesterday,
Yet bridges may rise anew,
Forged by bonds both strong and true.

Consumed by Flame

In the heart of fervent fire,
Desires dance and then expire,
Consume the night in burning glow,
Where secrets lie and shadows know.

From the spark that lights the blaze,
To the smokescreen's hazy gaze,
Flames devour what we hold dear,
Leaving ashes, cold and clear.

Yet in the ash, seeds may find,
Hopes reborn that bear the kind,
Flames may burn but dreams endure,
From the fire, life blooms pure.

Fury of the Elements

Winds howl beyond the quiet night,
Raging seas crash with might.
Thunder rumbles, skies ignite,
Nature's fury, primal, bright.

Mountains tremble, fears align,
Rivers swell, break confines.
Torrents flood, trees entwine,
Earth's raw power, all divine.

Storms will pass, calm restore,
Echoes linger evermore.
Lessons learned from nature's core,
Strength in bursts, life's grand tour.

Lightning pierces darkened skies,
In its flash, truth belies.
Heed the warnings, through the cries,
Elements speak with open eyes.

Embrace the tempest, fear aside,
In its wrath, wisdom resides.
Nature's dance, wild and wide,
In her fury, hearts confide.

Ablaze in Silence

Silent whispers through the flame,
Hearts ignite, none to blame.
Secrets burn, call your name,
In the quiet, passion's claim.

Eyes meet, no words reply,
Heat between, cannot deny.
In the glow, fires lie,
Unspoken love, fierce and sly.

Embers glow, soft and bright,
In the dark, pure delight.
Silent vows in gentle light,
Bound together, night after night.

Ashes fall, memories stay,
In the silence, find our way.
Flames of past, guiding ray,
Forever marked, come what may.

In the hush, hearts combine,
Love's true fire, pure design.
Silent blaze, ever mine,
In the quiet, spirits shine.

Combustion of Dreams

Dreams ignite in starlit skies,
Hopes take wing where courage flies.
In the night, visions rise,
Burning bright, through weary eyes.

Fears dissolve in passion's blaze,
Paths revealed, dreams amaze.
Steps we take, journeys phrase,
To the goals, endless praise.

Fire within, fuels our quest,
In the heart, dreams are blessed.
Through the trials, we invest,
In the hopes, we find our rest.

Every spark lights the way,
In the dark, beam of day.
Dreams on fire, find the say,
In the embered, we will stay.

In the roast, dreams unfold,
Souls entwined, brave and bold.
Burn and rise, stories told,
In the dreams, truths are sold.

Silent Inferno

In the quiet, flames ignite,
Raging strong, out of sight.
Burning deep into the night,
Silent roar, fierce and bright.

Hearts afire with no sound,
Love consumes, unbound.
In the hush, passion found,
Silent blaze, no rebound.

Eyes reflect the hidden heat,
Silent flames, quietly meet.
In this fire, hearts beat,
In the quiet, love's retreat.

Glowing embers softly speak,
In their warmth, we seek.
Silent truths, though weak,
Love's inferno, hearts streak.

In the still, we ignite,
Silent flames, pure delight.
Tied in fire, hand tight,
In the quiet, endless night.

Burnt Horizons

Beneath the endless stretch of sky,
The sun descends in ember glow.
A world ablaze with crimson sigh,
As twilight's flames begin to grow.

Mountains stand, their peaks on fire,
Silhouettes in the fading light.
Nature's pyre bids farewell,
To the languid arms of night.

Whispers in the cooling dusk,
Carry tales of warmth and flame.
The glowing edge of day's descent,
Marks the end of heaven's claim.

Now the night takes gentle hold,
Scorched by past and future fears.
Burnt horizons, stories told,
Through the veil of falling tears.

Searing Silence

In the hush of twilight's breath,
Words dissolve in molten air.
Stillness sears like burning death,
Scarring hearts beyond repair.

Lonely cries to heavens lost,
Echo through the flaming night.
Silence's searing, endless cost,
Hidden far from mortal sight.

Burning stars, celestial pyres,
Watch as world and soul ignite.
Searing silence, lost desires,
Cast in shadows of their flight.

Once a voice, now ember's wisp,
Gone to ash with silent scream.
In the searing silent grip,
All our dreams like smoke redeem.

Infernal Echoes

Amidst the shadows, echoes rise,
Flames that dance in night's embrace.
From the depths where fury lies,
Infernal whispers leave a trace.

Voices of a past on fire,
Haunt the corridors of mind.
Unseen specters of desire,
Embers lost, yet still they bind.

Through the chaos, through the burn,
Sorrows echo loud and clear.
All that's left with each return,
Is the heat of nameless fear.

Scorched by memories, they call,
Through the veils of smoke and dust.
Infernal echoes, one and all,
Fade to whispers, grey as rust.

Charred Whispers

In the heart of ashen woods,
Where the flames have left their mark.
Charred whispers tell of paths once good,
Now cast in eternal dark.

Branches, blackened by the blaze,
Murmur secrets to the night.
Once green leaves, in fiery haze,
Turn to cinders in their flight.

The forest speaks in tongues of old,
Language burnt, yet still it mourns.
Charred whispers of a story told,
Where every tree and root adorns.

Through the desolation's veil,
Tales of rebirth softly yearn.
Charred whispers in the wind's wail,
Promise life's eventual return.

Everlasting Ember

In twilight's grasp, the ember glows,
With whispers soft, it boldly shows,
A dance of light, fierce and warm,
    Surviving every storm.

The night is deep, the sky profound,
Yet ember's heart, a ceaseless sound,
Against the dark, it softly beams,
    Weaving through our dreams.

Through ages past, it stands so firm,
    In quietude, a potent germ,
Its fire's tale, though whispers may,
    Will light another day.

Flame's Lament

The flame, it weeps, its tears like dawn,
For fleeting loves, forever gone,
In ashes deep, where shadows play,
It yearns for brittle day.

A whispered woe, a torch's sigh,
Beneath the moon's indifferent eye,
It dances slow, with sorrow's grace,
A lament for time's embrace.

Each spark, a tear, each glow, a pain,
Across the hearth, a mournful strain,
In silent night, its voice is true,
A flame that aches for you.

Ashen Anthology

From fire's birth, the ashes fall,
A testament to life's recall,
In greys and whites, a story's told,
Of warmth that once was bold.

Each fragment here, a tale imbues,
Of passions lost, and transient views,
In hazy hues, existence speaks,
Of strong to silent peaks.

The wind, it lifts, the remnants high,
In clouds of memory to the sky,
An anthology in soot and dust,
Of things that fade, yet trust.

Ghosts of the Furnace

In furnace glow, where shadows spin,
Ghosts of flames once danced within,
Their whispers faint, like morning mist,
In memories, they persist.

The coals are dark, the fire's end,
But spirits of the warmth transcend,
They linger close, in still, deep air,
In dreams, they're everywhere.

With thoughts alight, these phantoms tread,
Upon the paths, where embers bled,
In silence, they forever blaze,
In mind's eternal haze.

Blazing Shadows

In twilight's bloom, the shadows dance,
A fiery hue in night's advance,
Embers flicker, secrets trace,
In darkness, light finds its embrace.

Whispers soft as night's design,
Stars above begin to shine,
Through the veil, a tale unfolds,
Mysteries in shadows bold.

Moonlight's glow on hidden streams,
Casts a spell of vivid dreams,
Silent echoes, unseen might,
Shadows blaze with spectral light.

Phoenix wings in evening's haze,
Ignite the night with gentle blaze,
Fading whispers, shadows deep,
Till dawn awakes from silent sleep.

In the dusk where echoes play,
Shadows keep the night at bay,
Blazing trails where time suspends,
In shadow's grip, the night transcends.

Amber Reverie

Golden hues in evening's breath,
Amber skies suspend past death,
Dreams entangle, time unwinds,
In this realm, the heart finds.

Sunset whispers to the soul,
Painted skies, an amber goal,
Touched by light that softly gleams,
Woven with the silk of dreams.

In this trance where spirits fly,
Light as feathers in the sky,
Voices soft as morning dew,
Whisper secrets old and new.

Silent rivers through the night,
Gleam beneath the star's delight,
Flowing gently to the sea,
In this amber reverie.

Moments stolen, hold them tight,
Memories of amber light,
In these dreams where worlds collide,
Amber skies our hearts confide.

Flame's Folly

In the hearth where fires burn,
Flame's folly takes its turn,
Dancing wild with reckless flair,
In the embers, secrets flare.

Whispers in the crackling night,
Flames that flicker, shadows bite,
In the midst of amber's glow,
Tales of old begin to flow.

Fire's folly, bright and bold,
A story in the night retold,
Through the ash and smoky screen,
Visions of the in-between.

Sparks that leap with joyous grace,
Trace the lines on time's own face,
In the blaze, a brief charade,
Lives that flicker, then they fade.

But within this flaming guise,
Lies a truth that never dies,
In the embers' soft embrace,
Find the dance of time and space.

Timbers of Time

In forests deep where silence reigns,
Timbers whisper through the chains,
Of time that weaves its endless thread,
Through leaves of green and autumn's red.

Roots that delve through ages past,
Ancient stories shadows cast,
In the wood, the years retold,
In rings where secrets gently hold.

Branches reach towards the sky,
Touch the stars where dreams lie,
In the sway of evening's grace,
Feel the breath of time's embrace.

Seasons change, yet still they stand,
Timbers shaped by nature's hand,
Silent sentinels they remain,
Guardians of the earth's domain.

Listen close, the timbers speak,
Wisdom in their quiet creak,
Through the years and endless climb,
Hear the song of the timbers of time.

Torchlight's Whisper

In the night's confined embrace,
A torch's whisper lights the lane,
Shadows dance in fleeting grace,
 Echoes of an ancient strain.

Flickering beams that softly kiss,
Walls that guard forgotten tales,
Through the mist, a sibilant hiss,
Guiding steps on time-worn trails.

Amber glimmers mark our path,
Silent guide through dusk's domain,
In its glow, we share our laughs,
Torchlight's whisper, never wanes.

Faint and soft, the flames do speak,
Of legends, love, and wraiths unseen,
In the quiet, secrets leak,
 From the fire's golden sheen.

As the night begins to fade,
Torchlight whispers still persist,
In our hearts, the dance portrayed,
By the flames that gently twist.

Consumed by Heat

In the core of summer's blaze,
Hearts ignited, spirits burn,
Each moment, a molten phase,
In the heat, our souls discern.

Crimson sky and fiery breath,
Nature scorched in passion's wake,
Burning fields of endless breadth,
In the warmth, our lives remake.

Sweat and sinew, glowing bright,
Underneath the sun's cruel gaze,
Every step, a test of might,
Consumed by heat, a fiery maze.

Every breath, a furnace deep,
Life ignited from the core,
In this realm, no want for sleep,
In the heat, we seek much more.

As the twilight cools the skin,
Whispering of day's defeat,
Still the passion burns within,
Forevermore, consumed by heat.

Singed Spirit

A phoenix rising from the pyre,
In the ashes, hope rebounds,
Spirit singed yet so inspired,
In the flame, its life resounds.

Every burn an ancient trial,
Marked by searing, holy brand,
In the fire, the mind defiles,
Then is cleansed by healing hand.

Fiery wings now stretch and strive,
Embers dance in joyous thrill,
In this blaze, the soul revived,
In the heat, it drinks its fill.

Scorched yet free, the spirit roams,
Through the cinders of the night,
In the fire, it finds its home,
Kindled by the burning light.

Rise, oh spirit, burnt yet whole,
Singed but bearing sacred scars,
In the blaze, renew your role,
In the flames, become the stars.

Blaze of Oblivion

In the heart of shadows deep,
Burning bright, the final flare,
Blaze of oblivion does seep,
Through the night's turbid air.

Hearts entwined in passion's fire,
In the end, they both consume,
In the flames of raw desire,
Turn to ash within the gloom.

Darkness wields its searing brand,
Smoldering dreams left to dust,
Blaze of oblivion's fierce hand,
Scorched remains of broken trust.

In the cinders, echoes wane,
Of a fire that once was bright,
Now the darkness will sustain,
In the void, extinguished light.

As the blaze does slowly die,
Memories fade, ember's end,
Blaze of oblivion, the sigh,
Of lost loves that shadows send.

Obsidian Burns

In shadows deep where silence yearns,
The heart of night, obsidian burns.
A whisper lost in a cavern's breath,
Eternal void, untouched by death.

Fire's echo in the darkened spire,
Embodied frost, imprisoned fire.
Mirror of stars with secrets sewn,
A darkened pulse, a heart of stone.

The sky reflects no mortal light,
Just endless depths of ancient night.
Embers cold that brightly gleam,
A silent scream, a shadowed dream.

Bones of darkness silently yearn,
For the dawn where days return.
But in this heart, obsidian stays,
Its fire cloaked in endless blaze.

Embrace of Ember

Through twilight's veil, the embers flare,
A warm embrace of autumn air.
Forgotten whispers cross the breeze,
In golden light through ancient trees.

Fingers trace a fire's edge,
Promises in spark's allege.
Whirling dance of ash and heat,
Where time and memory softly meet.

Fleeting moments quickly spent,
Years in embers' soft lament.
A heart once cold, now gently warms,
In ember's arms, the night transforms.

Glowing softly through the night,
A beacon of a past delight.
In every spark, a tale reborn,
In ember's embrace till dawn.

Forgotten Flames

In relics of a time long gone,
The flames of old still carry on.
A whisper in the desert sand,
A fire born in ancient land.

Remnants of a passion bright,
Whispered through the endless night.
Caretakers of a hidden past,
In each forgotten flame they last.

Ghosts of embers drift away,
In shadows where the memories lay.
Buried deep in silent ground,
Where histories in flames were found.

Echoes of a fire's glare,
Lingering in the quiet air.
Forgotten flames that gently burn,
A past awaiting its return.

Inferno's Memory

Beneath the ash, a story lies,
Of days consumed and darkened skies.
A blaze that danced with fierce delight,
Left shadows in the memory's light.

The inferno's roar, a haunting call,
Through time it echoes, past the wall.
A world reborn in crimson fire,
Dreams consumed in its desire.

Silent ruins, blackened stone,
Whispers of a past unknown.
In every cinder, every scar,
Lives the memory of a star.

Here the fire's spirit stays,
In twilight's end and dawn's new rays.
Inferno's memory, fierce and bright,
Eternal flame through endless night.

Crackle of Loneliness

In the quiet, shadows play,
Ghosts of yesteryears sway.
Echoes whisper, memories fray,
Amidst the silence, hearts lay.

Silent sobs shatter the night,
Moon's pale glow, cold light.
Stars above in distant flight,
Loneliness tightens its spite.

Broken dreams on the floor,
Hopes lost, love's no more.
Walls confining, like a sore,
Loneliness, a gripping bore.

Curtains drawn, world asks why,
Eyes stare, longing to cry.
Words unspoken, a mute lie,
Loneliness, a tear gone dry.

Endless days, nights of glass,
Time trickles, moments pass.
Inward sighs, outward masks,
Loneliness, a solemn caste.

Engulfed in Silence

Halls devoid of sound,
Stillness all around.
Echoes muted, profound,
Silence's depths unbound.

Night's embrace so cold,
Whispers left untold.
Empty arms to hold,
Silence's grip bold.

Eyes look but don't see,
Light fades gradually.
In shadows, spirits flee,
Silence, a somber melody.

Winds whisper through trees,
Nature's hushed pleas.
Calm spreads with ease,
Silence, a soft breeze.

In the void, thoughts drown,
Solitude, a heavy crown.
Yet peace in the quiet gown,
Silence, where dreams are sown.

Flame's Whisper

Candle flickers in night air,
Soft glow, warmth to share.
Shadows dance without care,
Flame's whisper, secrets rare.

Heat rises, stories unfold,
In its light, tales told.
Flickering threads, pure gold,
In flame's whisper, hearts bold.

Silent guardian in the dark,
Illuminates with a spark.
Guides lost souls, a tiny arc,
Flame's whisper, leaves a mark.

Burning brighter, never dies,
Reflecting in tired eyes.
Journey's end, or new highs,
Flame's whisper, softly cries.

In the hearth, dreams ignite,
Warm embrace through the night.
Flame's whisper casts its light,
Tender glow, pure delight.

Ashen Reveries

Dust settles, memories decay,
In grey hues, hopes lay.
Dreams of youth, gone astray,
Ashen reveries, endless fray.

Silent whispers in the winds,
Lost battles, silent sins.
Fortunes turned, fate grins,
Ashen reveries, new begins.

Once bright skies now dull,
Time's relentless pull.
History's weight so full,
Ashen reveries, hearts lull.

Forgotten paths, lifeless trees,
Eternal wait, stagnant seas.
Moments pass with ease,
Ashen reveries, gentle tease.

In the ashes, embers spark,
Fading light in the dark.
New flames, tiny mark,
Ashen reveries, hope's arc.

Among the Cinders

Amid the ash, where shadows creep,
A whispered tale in silence steeped,
Burnt remnants of a dream once strong,
In embered ruins, where we belong.

Ghostly figures 'neath the soot,
Forgotten pathways underfoot,
Memories smolder in the dusk,
As cinders drift like whispered husk.

Twilight's glow in fiery hues,
Hints of scarlet, smoky blues,
Through the haze, our spirits wander,
Among the cinders, hearts grow fonder.

Flakes of ash on wind's sigh,
Traces of the past float by,
Echoes of a world erased,
Among the cinders, time's embrace.

In the silence, hear the call,
Of lives that crumbled, chose to fall,
Yet 'midst the ashes, find our place,
Among the cinders, endless grace.

Phoenix Tears

From the flame, a tear does fall,
A symbol of the phoenix's call,
Glowing brightly in the night,
Transforming sorrow into light.

Ancient cries aloft the skies,
Where the wounded phoenix flies,
Healing power in its tears,
Vanquishing the darkest fears.

Renewal born from fiery end,
Tears like jewels, a hope they send,
Through the ashes, rise anew,
With every drop, a journey true.

Fires fade yet they ignite,
Brilliance borne from endless night,
In those tears, a promise lies,
From embers, flames will rise.

For every tear, the phoenix weeps,
A soul awakened gently sleeps,
In rebirth's tender, sunlit beams,
Phoenix tears and newfound dreams.

Beyond the Inferno

Through the wall of scorching heat,
A brighter future we shall meet,
Beyond the inferno's raging might,
Awaits a world bathed in light.

Flames may roar and shadows leer,
Yet hope remains, crystal clear,
In the furnace, hearts withstand,
For beyond, there's promised land.

Through the embers, pathways weave,
Roads of gold and turns that cleave,
Journey forth with spirits bold,
Beyond the fire, tales unfold.

Burnished skies and molten streams,
Hold within the dreams we dream,
Touch the stars, extinguish fear,
Beyond the inferno, draw near.

Pass the gate of flame unbowed,
Rise above the searing shroud,
In the light of dawn's sweet kiss,
Beyond the inferno, endless bliss.

Echoes of the Blaze

In the heart of flames so high,
Voices whisper, breathe a sigh,
Echoes of a burning blaze,
Chanting through the fire's haze.

Flickering light on ashen ground,
Memories in flames profound,
Every spark, a tale retold,
As echoes of the blaze unfold.

Crackling timber, twilight's song,
In the blaze, where shadows throng,
Blazing pyres, stories rise,
Etched in embered, fiery skies.

Silent whispers in the heat,
Of the past, where kindred meet,
Ghostly calls through time's maze,
Hear the echoes of the blaze.

From the ashes, life regresses,
Void of flames, the earth confesses,
Yet in hearts, the fire stays,
Living echoes of the blaze.

Cinders of Dream

In twilight's gentle, fleeting gleam,
A whisper calls through endless night,
Embers dance in soft moonbeam,
Carrying hopes in fragile light.

Ashes swirl in dreams' embrace,
Shadows cast by silent flame,
Memories rise without a trace,
Yet no two nights are quite the same.

Flickering phantoms stretch and wane,
Within the heart, a burning glow,
From coldest depths to heights insane,
Where wishes dare to feel and grow.

Cinders whisper secrets deep,
In realms of dusk where longing lies,
Awakening those who seek to keep,
The dreams that live in closed eyes.

An ember's sigh, the night concludes,
Scattering sparks of silent scream,
As morning's light the dark intrudes,
To reignite each cinder's dream.

Heatwave Haze

Beneath the sun's relentless blaze,
A world unfolds in liquid air,
Mirages drift in heatwave haze,
Reality shimmers, lightens, and tears.

The ground beneath, a canvas wide,
Patterns swirl in tingling light,
Whispers in the warmth abide,
Painting daydreams, blazing bright.

Shadows shrink, escape the sun,
Every breath a weighted sigh,
Day and night converge as one,
Underneath the molten sky.

Moments melt in summer's hold,
Time drips past in languid flow,
Stories told in flames and gold,
In heat's embrace, we come to know.

Sweat and hope in fevered chase,
Drifting through the glaring maze,
We seek the calm in summer's face,
Lost within the heatwave haze.

Torched Reflections

A blaze ignites within the glass,
Echoes sing in crimson light,
Reflections dance, then swiftly pass,
Torching shadows in their flight.

Flames reveal and flames obscure,
Truth and lies in swirling hues,
In mirror's depths, the burning pure,
Shows the self and phantom views.

Glimmers mark the soul's true face,
Where shadows once in silence stood,
Fire's breath in quiet grace,
Brings forth tales of bad and good.

From embered depths, reflections rise,
A story etched in glowing fire,
Hints of truth in flickered guise,
Reveal the heart's deep desire.

As dawn breaks through the smoky veil,
Reflections cool in morning's breath,
The torch, now spent, leaves just a trail,
Of dreams reborn from night's rough death.

Pyre of the Past

Beneath the stars' eternal gaze,
A pyre burns in solemn night,
Casting memories in its blaze,
Turning shadows into light.

Flames consume the days gone by,
Ashes dance to silent song,
In their flight, the whispers lie,
O'er the past where we belong.

Each ember holds a whispered tale,
Of joy and sorrow intertwined,
In pyre's glow, the spirits trail,
Stories left within the mind.

From the flames, the dreams ascend,
Scattered like the stardust vast,
Yet in heart, they find an end,
In the pyre of the past.

Morning breaks, the ashes cool,
Where flames once held their vibrant fast,
In the dawn, we find the fuel,
To craft the fire that will last.

Elemental Elegy

Earth and sky, a rhythmic dance,
Swirling winds in wild romance.
Mountains whisper, oceans weep,
Secrets hidden, shadows creep.

Fire's fury, water's grace,
Ancient echoes, time's embrace.
Air's caress, the storm's decree,
Nature's song, forever free.

Sunrise paints the dawn anew,
Moonlight drapes the night in blue.
Stars like jewels, distant, bright,
Infinite realms in boundless flight.

Whispers carried on the breeze,
Leaves that tremble, spirits tease.
In the stillness, life's refrain,
Elemental, unchained domain.

Through the tempest, through the calm,
Nature holds its own sweet charm.
Every heartbeat, every sigh,
Elemental, soars the sky.

Conflagration's Call

Flames that dance in evening's hue,
Crimson gold, a vivid view.
Woodlands whisper, sparks ignite,
Fire's embrace, a fierce delight.

Blazing trails through night and day,
Ancient forests melt away.
Wild and raging, untamed call,
Nature's fury, fierce enthrall.

Embers glow, a soft refrain,
Echoes of the storm's remain.
Cinders scatter, ashes fall,
Conflagration's echo, primal call.

Waves of heat that rise and sway,
Night turns swiftly into day.
Through the darkness, fiery gleam,
Dreams consumed in burning seam.

Yet from ashes life can rise,
Phoenix born beneath the skies.
In destruction's fervent wake,
New beginnings fires make.

Pyre's Promise

Through the gloom, a light persists,
In the shadows, hope insists.
Flickering flames, a beacon bright,
Guiding souls through darkest night.

Candles flicker, whispers trace,
Every glow, a warm embrace.
Spirits lifted by the spark,
Piercing through the deepest dark.

Smoke ascends, a silver veil,
In its tendrils, stories sail.
Whispers carried far and wide,
Promises in fire's stride.

Bold and fierce, yet calmly still,
Flame that bends to timeless will.
In its ardor, dreams are spun,
Every shadow, every sun.

As the pyre burns to ash,
Sparks disperse in sudden flash.
With each ember, life's decree,
Infinite, our legacy.

Light into Shadows

Morning sun, a golden blaze,
Chasing night with gilded rays.
Through the mist, the world awakes,
Light into shadows softly breaks.

Crimson dawn, the skies aflame,
Colors whisper, call your name.
In the stillness, day unfolds,
Secret tales the light beholds.

Sunsets paint the heavens wide,
Hues that blush as day subsides.
Twilight calls, a gentle sweep,
Light into shadows' tender keep.

Stars emerge in velvet skies,
Hints of wonder in their eyes.
Moonlight bathes the world in dreams,
Softly, through the night it streams.

Light descends, and shadows grow,
Evening's hush in softest glow.
In the dance of night and day,
Light into shadows fades away.

Through the Fire's Veil

Flames dance in twilight's soft embrace,
Bright tongues that flicker, twist, and sway.
Through ember's glow and shadowed trace,
A world in orange and crimson play.

Beneath the canopy of stars,
The fire reveals its fiery lore.
Whispers of ancient, distant scars,
Echoes of battles fought before.

Golden sparks that leap and chase the moon,
Weaving tales of courage and fear.
In every flicker lies a secret tune,
A melody for those who dare to hear.

Warmth and light from night's dark crown,
Bursts of wonder in each flare.
Guided by the fire's gown,
Journeys start in its radiant glare.

Through the veil of burning dreams,
Mysteries past and future blend.
In the flames, a life redeems,
A circle with no darkened end.

Burned Essence

In the heart of blazing might,
Essence pure, by heat laid bare.
Truths obscured by blinding light,
Whispered secrets in the air.

Smoke curls upward, grace in gray,
Lifted prayers to the night stars.
Melting layers of ancient clay,
Revealing selves, letting down guards.

Ashes fall like memory's snow,
Grey dust of what once stood so tall.
From the ruins new dreams grow,
Phoenix embers heed the call.

In the scorch of daylight's gaze,
Burned essence finds its form anew.
Out of fire, through the haze,
A spirit born, both wild and true.

By the forge of life's hot hand,
Shaped and tempered, molded bright.
Strengthened in the fiery land,
Soul emerged from darkest night.

Through the Ashes

Walk the path where shadows fall,
Ashes whisper tales of old.
Silent echoes, spirits call,
In their depths, new truths unfold.

Footprints mark the sooty ground,
Steps once taken, dreams once known.
In the quiet, heartbeats pound,
Through the ashes, seeds are sown.

Life reduced to dust and grey,
Yet in cinders, hope ignites.
Every dusk gives birth to day,
Flickers turning into lights.

Past the remnants of despair,
Glimmers of tomorrow gleam.
In the stillness of the air,
Whispers weave the strangest dream.

Through the ashes, look and see,
Moments lost but not in vain.
In their fall lies destiny,
Born in tears, washed by rain.

Embers of Memory

Among the coals of yesteryears,
Embers glow with a soft light.
In their warmth, forgotten fears,
Fade into the embrace of night.

Memories spark, an amber glow,
Flickering scenes of distant lands.
Moments past, like rivers flow,
Through the heart's remembering sands.

Tales of love and days gone by,
Burn within this gentle pyre.
Stories etched upon the sky,
Woven from the threads of fire.

Whispers in the ember's hue,
Songs of laughter, cries of woe.
In their dance, both old and new,
Life's fleeting essence starts to show.

Embers of what once had been,
Guardians of a timeless lore.
In their glow, the eyes have seen,
History's light forevermore.

Unquenched Yearning

Upon the shore where dreams reside,
The waves caress, yet hearts divide,
The moon whispers a lover's plea,
In silent night, we yearn to see.

A star falls swift, a wish in flight,
A glimmer in the endless night,
Yet shadows cast by longing's light,
Bind us in eternal plight.

Beneath the sky, so vast and grand,
Our footsteps trace the silver sand,
In every breeze, your name we find,
A haunting echo in our mind.

Through time and space, we drift apart,
Bound by the chains of aching heart,
Unquenched the thirst, forever more,
Forbidden love's unclosing door.

Oh, fleeting moments, whispers lost,
In twilight's grip, we count the cost,
Of yearning's flame that burns unseen,
Forever caught in love's between.

Tempest of Flames

A tempest brews in fiery skies,
With thunder's roar and lightning's cries,
The world ignites in fierce refrain,
As passion storms like untamed rain.

The wind, it howls with wild despair,
As embers dance upon the air,
And in the blaze, our souls entwine,
Two hearts forged in infernal shrine.

Each whisper fuels the growing fire,
Desire's breath as wild as wire,
Consumed within this ardent dance,
Amidst the flames of reckless chance.

With eyes ablaze and spirits torn,
We face the dawn, a love reborn,
In this tempest, fierce and bright,
We find our strength within the light.

But as the storm begins to wane,
We bear the scars of love's fierce reign,
In memory's glow, the fire tames,
The lasting heat of tempest flames.

Evaporated Echo

In quiet rooms where shadows fall,
An echo lingers, faint and small,
A whisper soft of days gone by,
Now swept away like summer sky.

The voices fade, the laughter still,
Like morning dew on distant hill,
Emotions rise, then drift apart,
An echo's ghost inside the heart.

Splintered dreams and memories,
Float away on gentle breeze,
Unseen, unheard, they gently go,
In silent streams, they ebb and flow.

Yet in the hush of night alone,
Their presence felt, their spirits known,
An echo lingers, bittersweet,
Of moments lost and incomplete.

As time slips by, the echoes wane,
Yet in our hearts, they still remain,
A fleeting touch, a spectral glow,
The lasting trace of echo's show.

Flicker of Forsaken

Amidst the gloom where shadows creep,
A flicker dances in the deep,
A whispered tale of love once known,
Now stands as ghost, forever lone.

The flames that burned so bright, so hot,
Now flicker weak with dreams forgot,
In silence cold, the ember's sigh,
A lingering pain as moments die.

Once fervent vows and hearts ablaze,
Now lost within the twilight haze,
Forgotten paths and whispered names,
Scattered ashes of forsaken flames.

In twilight's grasp, we seek the past,
Yet find a love that could not last,
The flicker fades, but leaves behind,
A haunting trace within the mind.

Though time may pass and wounds may mend,
The flicker of forsaken's end,
Lingers on in darkest night,
A phantom's glow, a lost love's light.

Molten Farewells

In fields of molten farewells, we part,
The sun sets low, a flaming start.
Ash whispers secrets to the night,
As shadows flee the dwindling light.

Crimson skies paint a somber hue,
Echoing dreams we once knew.
Embers drift in sorrow's haze,
In silent dance, our final blaze.

The earth sighs, with scorching breath,
Marking end with signs of death.
Resigned to fate, we face the pyre,
Love's remnants in the endless fire.

Tears evaporate in twilight's glow,
Farewells forged in burning woe.
A fleeting touch, a quiet weep,
As we dissolve into night's deep.

Through molten paths, our spirits wade,
In shadows, distant promises fade.
A silent vow, to once return,
From ashes of this painful burn.

Shade of the Conflagration

In the shade of the conflagration's roar,
We stand united, hearts no more.
Flames reflect in eyes worn thin,
A battle rages deep within.

Smoke serpentines through fractured skies,
Unveiling truths, unmasking lies.
Through ashen veils, we stride ahead,
Chasing echoes of words unsaid.

The ground beneath, a blazing sea,
Molten whispers call to thee.
In fervent heat, our shadows blend,
Boundless fires, a twisted friend.

Stars retreat from fiery blight,
Melding day with darkest night.
Yet through the blaze, we rise unscathed,
Forged anew, in wrath we bathe.

The heart of fire, a grim embrace,
In shadows strong, with steeled grace.
Emerging past the fiery scorn,
From ash and shade, reborn, reborn.

Radiant Sanction

Beneath the glow of radiant sanction's reach,
We seek the truths within its breach.
Golden beams caress the air,
In light's embrace, we find repair.

Fleeting hours, marked by sun's cast,
Moments held, and yet they pass.
In the gleam of dawn's first kiss,
Lies the promise of our bliss.

Arcs of light, in spectral dance,
Ignite the heart, with fervent trance.
Shadows bow in night's retreat,
To morning's call, so pure, so sweet.

Each ray a bond, in warmth conveyed,
Sanctioned bright, in bond unweighed.
To golden hues, our spirits leap,
In light's embrace, our hearts to keep.

In radiant warmth, we find our way,
Through brilliant dawn to end of day.
Sanctioned by the light divine,
Together bound, in endless shine.

Grasping at Smoke

In the fleeting mist, we grasp at smoke,
Chasing dreams in whispered cloak.
Phantoms dance on twilight's edge,
Evading hold though hands do pledge.

Through smoky veils, our past concealed,
In wisp of memory, truth revealed.
Ephemeral thoughts in darkness glide,
In shadows deep, our souls reside.

A breath, a sign, the moment slips,
Through fingers' grasp, like gossamer tips.
We seek the form of what was near,
Yet find it gone, like morning's tear.

In twilight's grasp, we search in vain,
For echoes of forgotten pain.
The smoke evades, a ghostly jest,
Leaving hearts in silent quest.

Yet in the chase, we find our peace,
In smoke's embrace, our doubts release.
Grasping not, but letting go,
We find the truth in airy flow.

Smoldering Secrets

In shadows dark, where whispers creep,
Beneath the secrets that we keep.
Flickering truth in flames of night,
A hidden world just out of sight.

Smokescreen lies in ember's glow,
Masked intentions never show.
Silent vows and hushed confessions,
Burn in quiet, darkened sessions.

Veiled mysteries ignite the past,
Memories that could not last.
Through the haze of silent screams,
Secrets melt our fractured dreams.

From the ashes rise anew,
Stories that we never knew.
As the flames consume the dark,
Smoldering secrets leave their mark.

In the remnants of the blaze,
Fleeting moments lost in daze.
Echoes of what once was real,
Now dissolve in silent zeal.

Burnt Pages

Burnt pages of forgotten tales,
Blown by winds like ghostly sails.
Each word consumed by fiery kiss,
Eternal loss of whispered bliss.

In ashen depths of charred remains,
Lie the echoes of our pains.
Lines once penned in love's pure flame,
Now erased from time's cruel game.

Flames of sorrow dance so high,
In night's embrace, they light the sky.
Tears of ink now cease to flow,
Burnt pages hint at what we know.

Stories etched in heart and mind,
Now in smoke are left behind.
Melancholy fills the air,
Lost to embers, tales laid bare.

From the cinders rise anew,
A phoenix born in fiery hue.
Burnt pages of our past regrets,
In fire, we forge new thoughts and sets.

Glow of Abandonment

In the cold and silent night,
Glows a flame frail yet bright.
Abandoned dreams in ember's sway,
Rekindle whisper of the day.

Lonely sparks in twilight's hall,
Yearn for voices, silent call.
Echoes of a past once near,
Fading fast, consumed by fear.

Glow of hopes now left behind,
Pale their light in shadowed mind.
Flicker softly, time has flown,
In the dark, they burn alone.

From the ashes, rise or fall,
Memories stand but shadows tall.
Glow of loss, yet hearts still yearn,
In the embers, lessons learn.

In the night, the fire plays,
Casting light on yesterdays.
Glow of abandonment endures,
Quiet, still, as hope ensures.

Fiery Epiphany

In the heart of deepest night,
Blazed a sudden, brilliant light.
Fiery thought from ashes grew,
Revelation sharp and true.

Burning bright, the mind transforms,
Fires of change, the soul rewarms.
Epiphany in flames divine,
Sparked by muses' silent sign.

From the flames, old chains release,
In their place, a newfound peace.
Cleansing fires of insight pure,
Guide us through, our paths assure.

Hearts ignite with fervent ease,
Melting fear like winter's freeze.
Fiery truth in each caress,
Wisdom gained we now confess.

In the ember's glow, a start,
Lessons forge within the heart.
Fiery epiphany, our guide,
Through the darkness, by our side.

Kindred Flames

In twilight's gentle, waning light,
Two souls ignite in boundless flight.
Their sparks, a dance that never wanes,
A harmony in life's domains.

Through storm and calm, they intertwine,
Embers of love, a sacred sign.
Unwavering, their bond sustains,
A fire eternal, free from chains.

Whispered dreams in midnight's hold,
Their warmth, a story yet untold.
Kindred flames through darkened skies,
A love that burns, and never dies.

Substantial Sparks

In shadows cast by fleeting time,
Two sparks ignite, a perfect rhyme.
Their brilliance shines through darkest night,
A beacon of defiant light.

In moments brief, yet ever bright,
They chase away the looming night.
A flash of wonder, brief yet grand,
An ode to what they understand.

Substantial sparks in voids of black,
A testament to courage's track.
They blaze, then fade, but always leave,
A trace of hope one can believe.

Inferno's Tale

In depths of earth where shadows creep,
A tale of fire begins to seep.
Inferno's whispers, echoes old,
A saga vast and yet untold.

From molten core to surface bright,
It weaves through day and endless night.
A tapestry of flame and lore,
A legend whispered evermore.

Through ages past, with fury's might,
It shapes the world, it fuels the fight.
Inferno's tale, both fierce and grand,
A story carved in molten sand.

Gleaming Ashes

In dawn's embrace, the ashes gleam,
A sight surreal, like fragile dream.
From fire's end, new life unfolds,
A phoenix tale of courage bold.

Beneath the soot, the ember's glow,
A promise of what life bestows.
Gleaming ashes, silent lore,
A whisper of what came before.

Through cycles vast of rise and fall,
They stand as witness, they recall.
In gleaming dust, past joys and smashes,
Hope reborn in gleaming ashes.

Fumer of Fantasies

In twilight's gentle, whispered song,
Where shadows dance and dreams belong,
A fumer breathes intents unknown,
Crafting realms where thoughts are sown.

Through realms of mist and willow wisp,
In visions sharp as lover's kiss,
He molds the stars with hands unseen,
In murmur's shade and midnight sheen.

Eclipsed by echoes, faint and near,
He weaves through webs of hope and fear,
Silent seer of slumber's shore,
Eternal sculptor, dream's encore.

In twilit threads where moonbeams lay,
He fashions night from dusk to day,
A phantom's craft in velvet skies,
Where fantasies in vapor rise.

His breath creates nocturnal blooms,
Alive in dark, embroidered rooms,
Oh fumer, wake the sleeping heart,
From night's embrace, to dreams we chart.

Blistering Waves

Upon the shore where tempests rage,
The sea's eternal, weathered stage,
Blistering waves in torment swell,
In brine and fury's endless spell.

They crash and roar, a beast untamed,
In foamy crests and salt unclaimed,
A symphony of rage and grace,
In storm's embrace, their endless chase.

The seagulls cry in wild refrain,
Above the thrashing, boiling plain,
Where shipwrecked hopes and driftwood lie,
Beneath the storm-bewitched sky.

Yet, in their anger, beauty grows,
As moonlit tides in silence flow,
Receding back to ocean's heart,
On journeys mystical, they start.

Upon this stage of ebb and tide,
With nature's strength and power allied,
Blistering waves, relentless play,
In dusk's embrace, another day.

Incendiary Silence

In quiet realms where hush prevails,
A spark ignites in voiceless gales,
Incendiary silence glows,
In whispered flames where secrets flow.

Each breath a blaze of hidden fire,
Unspoken words of fierce desire,
Volcanoes deep beneath the calm,
In silence, scorching midnight's psalm.

Night's cloak of stillness, draped and wide,
Conceals the embers tucked inside,
A world alight, yet soundless, bare,
With burning thoughts hung in the air.

Beneath the quiet, rivers flame,
A dance of fire without a name,
In mute embrace, the tongues of heat,
Transform the dark in sheer deceit.

Incendiary, the silence thrives,
In echoes of our quiet lives,
A smoldering serenade unseen,
Within the hush, where hearts convene.

Molten Memories

In caverns deep where shadows play,
Old memories in silence stay,
Like liquid gold, in twilight gleam,
They flow within a molten stream.

Past echoes fused in glowing ember,
In heart's forge we still remember,
Each role of time, each fleeting glance,
Preserved through love, a timeless dance.

The forge of souls, in heat and strife,
Cast memories' mold in ceaseless life,
Where passion, pain, and joy converge,
In molten realms, emotions surge.

Through ages past, the moments burn,
In ash and flame, the lessons learn,
A tapestry of times once lived,
In molten currents, they are sieved.

In cherish'd fire, these visions rest,
Against our hearts, they're ever pressed,
Molten memories, bright and bold,
Carved in our souls like ancient gold.

Glimmer of Forgotten Dreams

In the quiet of moonlit beams,
Whispers travel through the night.
Shadows dance in fleeting streams,
Glimmers of dreams taking flight.

Lost in time, these dreams once gold,
Now mere echoes of the past.
In their glow, tales of old,
Fragile, fleeting, gone too fast.

The stars above, silent and wise,
Keepers of forgotten lore.
In their twinkle, secrets rise,
Of dreams that are no more.

Yet within each heart's deep core,
Lingers glimmers faint but true.
Forgotten dreams forever soar,
In the night, in me and you.

Past the realms of sight and sound,
Where the heart and soul convene.
There forgotten dreams are found,
In their glimmer, evergreen.

Charcoal Memories

In the flicker of candle's grace,
Charcoal marks trace stories told.
Lines of time on a wrinkled face,
Memories in fingers old.

Artists' visions cast in gray,
Moments etched in life's own hue.
Shadows whisper, night and day,
Of the past and what we knew.

Every stroke a heartbeat's flame,
Breathing life into the void.
Charcoal whispers call my name,
In the silence, I am buoyed.

From the ashes, dreams arise,
In the dark a light is found.
Charcoal memories in disguise,
Speak in tones both soft and profound.

In the twilight's soft embrace,
Echoes linger, softly framed.
Charcoal sketches hold their place,
In our hearts forever named.

Flickers of Silence

In the midst of shadowed calm,
Where whispers dare not tread.
Silence sings a secret psalm,
In the space where words have fled.

Flickers of a timeless mood,
Dance on edges thin and brief.
Silent tales in solitude,
Speak in silence, bring relief.

In the void where echoes fade,
Silent flickers paint their tune.
In the stillness, truth is laid,
Underneath a silver moon.

Moments bound by quiet grace,
Hold the whispers of the night.
In the silence, we embrace,
Flickers soft and pure as light.

Through the hush of twilight's seam,
Where the heart and shadows meet.
Flickers of a silent dream,
In the silence, sound is sweet.

When the Heat Subsides

When the heat of day is past,
And the air begins to still.
Evening shadows lengthen fast,
Upon the cool and quiet hill.

Whispers of a gentle breeze,
Rustle leaves and soothe the mind.
Heat subsides, the world at ease,
In the twilight, peace we find.

Colors fade to shades of gray,
Stars awaken in the sky.
Daylight's fervor slips away,
Night's calm certainty is nigh.

In the stillness, hearts revive,
Breathing in the night's embrace.
When the heat no longer strives,
Softly, life resumes its pace.

As the darkness cloaks the land,
And the stars begin their glide.
We find solace hand in hand,
In the peace when heat subsides.

Embers of Farewell

In twilight's gentle, quiet fall,
The day takes its final bow.
Embers of farewell softly call,
As night descends, we wonder how.

Stars emerge, a delicate thread,
We weave our dreams in their glow.
Whispers of the things unsaid,
In the ember's silent flow.

Memories linger in the air,
A dance of light and shadow's play.
Each ember a moment shared,
Before it's gently swept away.

The night holds stories yet to tell,
In the silent, loving dark.
We'll meet again, who can foretell,
In another ember's spark.

So with the night, we softly blend,
In the embers of farewell.
Hoping for the light to mend,
And bring a dawn where love will swell.

Whispers in the Flames

In the hearth, where warmth resides,
Flames dance in a tender waltz.
Secret whispers, the fire confides,
In the silence, no one halts.

Crackling tales of olden times,
Ember stories, softly told.
Against the night, a thousand rhymes,
As flames embrace, fierce and bold.

Flickering dreams upon the logs,
Moments lost, yet never gone.
Voices hide within the fogs,
As the night slowly moves on.

In each fire, a heart does beat,
Lives entwined in burning glow.
Stories shared by spirits meet,
In whispers only flames can know.

As the night winds gently blow,
And the flames begin to wane.
Whispers in the flames, they flow,
Until only ash remains.

Dancing Shadows

On the walls, the shadows play,
Moving with the fire's grace.
In the dark, they softly sway,
Each one a secret to embrace.

They tell of worlds beyond our sight,
In their dance, a hidden lore.
Mysteries of the silent night,
In every shadow's whisper, more.

Figures fleeting, a phantom's spin,
Echoes of what once has been.
In their dance, the veil wears thin,
Moments caught in shadow's sheen.

Eyes alight with shadowed dreams,
Lost in every flicker's lore.
In the dark, a silken seam,
We weave through the shadow's door.

So we watch and so we wonder,
What these shadows seek to share.
In their dance, we lose and ponder,
All the secrets hidden there.

Ashes of Yesterday

In the stillness of the dawn,
Ashes whisper tales so old.
Songs of days now dead and gone,
Stories in the embers told.

Once-flamed passions, fierce and bright,
Now lie quiet, soft and grey.
Echoes of the endless night,
Ashes of our yesterday.

In the dust, a dream now found,
Fragments lost to time's own play.
Silent whispers all around,
Remnants of another day.

From the ashes, we arise,
Phoenix hearts that dare to soar.
In the glow of morning skies,
Newborn dreams forevermore.

So we take the ashes too,
In our hearts, their lessons stay.
For in the past, we find the true,
In the ashes of yesterday.

Veil of Smoke

Through forests deep and ancient night,
A cloak of darkness, chilling fright,
A whisper soft, the embers spoke,
Wrapped in the veil, a drifting smoke.

Shadows dance in eerie light,
Under skies, both black and bright,
Mysteries with each breath invoke,
Lost in the veil, a silent stroke.

Wisps of memory, ghosts afloat,
In a sea where sorrows bloat,
A fleeting touch, the world awoke,
Held by the veil, a sacred yoke.

Silent echoes the stars do stoke,
Binding dreams in fragile cloak,
A realm where only secrets poke,
Veiled in smoke, no words revoke.

Paths unseen by hopeful folk,
Through the veil, the past unspoke,
Journey long where spirits soak,
In the veil of smoke, evoking woke.

Sacred Blaze

In the heart of night, a flame does rise,
Painting gold the ebon skies,
Whispers turn to fervent cries,
Within the sacred, fire's guise.

Flickers dance on timbers old,
Narratives of legends told,
Scarlet tongues, their tales unfold,
In sacred blaze, we behold.

Through the dark their warmth conveys,
Echoes of eternal praise,
Embers sing in fiery maze,
A hallowed light, the sacred blaze.

Mystic incantations haze,
Shadows' sway in solemn plays,
Hopes and dreams the blaze conveys,
In the sacred night, it stays.

Rituals of ancient days,
Through the ember's tender phase,
A guiding light when vision strays,
Ever in the sacred blaze.

Doused Hope

In the quiet, rain descends,
Shrouding light as twilight bends,
Dreams once bright begin to blend,
Doused in hope that never mends.

Silent whispers, broken lines,
Echo through the stormy signs,
Each drop falls, a heart defines,
Hope doused in the rain's confines.

Wishing wells and silent prayers,
Lost within the cloudy layers,
As the thunder's anger flares,
Hope is doused, despair ensnares.

Muted cries, unspoken pleas,
Blended with the autumn breeze,
Every tear the soul will seize,
Doused in hope like fallen leaves.

Darkened skies, the storm's embrace,
Once bright glow in shadowed place,
Through the rain, a soft disgrace,
Hope doused hearts lose their race.

Flame-Spun Fantasies

In the glow of hearth's embrace,
Fantasies weave in their grace,
Flames that dance in cosmic space,
Whisper dreams where none can trace.

Magic swirls in amber hues,
Casting shades of mystic blues,
Every spark a life imbues,
Flame-spun dreams the heart pursues.

Tales of wonder, fire's art,
Ignite passion from the start,
Born from flames, the stories chart,
In the fantasy, play their part.

Twisting through an endless night,
Guardian dreams in soft twilight,
Each a thread of burning bright,
In flame-spun realms, they take flight.

Woven dreams from cinder's gaze,
Drawing paths through smoky haze,
In the dance of fire's blaze,
Flame-spun fantasies ever amaze.

Kindling Despair

Embers flicker, kindling despair
Waves of sorrow fill the air
Silent whispers lost in breeze
Heartaches grow with subtle ease

Veins encircle, tightly pressed
Breaking cries escape the chest
Burning softly, buried deep
Smoldering fires steal our sleep

Shadows dance upon the walls
In empty rooms, the darkness calls
In every smile, a hidden tear
The moments pass, consumed by fear

Leaves turn brown and skies turn gray
Night envelopes, consumes the day
Dreams of solace slowly fade
Despair's ember never swayed

Infernal Reverie

Eyes ablaze with untold fire
Whispers sing of dark desire
Lost within the dream's embrace
Fiery rhythms in empty space

Cosmic flames engulf the night
Books of fate, their pages bright
Vivid dreams of distant lands
Burning sands through endless hands

Ashen skies and swirling mist
Echoes from the shadows kissed
Haunted visions, midnight's call
In infernal reveries we fall

Timeless heat consumes our souls
Every inch, a fiery stroll
Waking worlds in smoky haze
Ever lost in fervent blaze

Blazing Solitude

Standing still in endless flame
Loneliness without a name
Silent cries in molten streams
Long-lost whispers, shattered dreams

Blazing sun in empty sky
In this furnace, tears run dry
Echoes faint within the heat
Burning paths this heart has beat

Barren landscapes stretch afar
Lonely like a fallen star
Scarlet shades on baked terrain
In the solitude, remain

Silent embers slowly die
Conflagration, last goodbye
Hope alight with one reprieve
Burning urge to still believe

Scorched Earth

Land beneath our weary feet
Scorched and cracked from summer's heat
Dust and ashes fill the air
All that's green, beyond repair

Forests burned to black, charred bone
Mountains high, like fire-thrown
Rivers dried, no life to see
Nature's groan in agony

Fields once lush, now desolate
Scars of fire, a cruel fate
Songs of life now turned to cries
Scorched earth beneath the burning skies

Whispers of a cooler past
Gone too quick, the die is cast
Hope is but a fleeting breath
In the arms of fiery death

Milton Keynes UK
Ingram Content Group UK Ltd.
UKHW050029190624
444315UK00015B/847

9 789916 756430